Sic Transit

Poems

Howard Bray

New Wine Press || 2015

11/18/20

*For Danny and Louise
with appreciation from a new
member of the Micah family.*

Howard

About the Author

Howard Bray is the author of *The Pillars of The Post* (Norton). His articles have appeared in *The New York Times Magazine*, *The Progressive*, and other magazines. He lives in Washington, DC.

Appreciation: *My gratitude for their support and encouragement as these poems evolved: Bea Harwood; Meredith Hadaway; Judy Viorst; John Bray; Ralph Widner; Effie and John Walsh, Buck Downs and, forever, Ann.*

Sic Transit ©2015 Howard Bray
ISBN # 978-1-312898-69-1
Cover Design by Jacob Bray
Book Design by Buck Downs

New Wine Press || Washington, DC
newwinepress@dcemail.com
To order additional copies, visit our product page at Lulu:
http://goo.gl/fPDDcm

Table of Contents

Free-Range	1
Geography	2
Apples	3
Sea of Corn	5
Usage	6
Spanish	7
Brick Work	8
McAvoy & Sons	9
The Med Student	11
September Song	12
First of January	13
Man on the Porch	14
Make Believe	15
Encoded	16
Judgment	17
The Little Lizard	18
Old San Juan	19
Penmanship	20
A Matter of Vowels	21
Confluence	22
Evidence of Love	23
Maui	24
The Dancer	25
Loggerheads	26
Masts	27
Navigation	28
Crossing Bay Bridge	29
Birthday Girl	30
Tightrope Walking	31

The Oak	32
Ambience	33
Along the River	34
Crew	35
Social Media	36
A Cat Tale	37
Max	38
Phone Call	39
Home Ec	40
Catching Flies	41
Obit	42
City Limits	43
Yard Sale	44
The DC-3	45
Conducting Heat	46
Cadence	47
Dover	49
Arlington Section 60	50
Faces	51
Sic Transit	52
Stone Saints	53
Prayer	54
Aridzona	55
Public Library	56
Two A.M.	58

Sic Transit

Free-Range

At the weekly farmers' market
lush with exurban bounty
on this late summer Sunday
in front of a tarp-roofed stand
shading a row of blue ice chests
my blithe fourth-grader points to the sign, asking,
"What's a free-range chicken?"

Feeling playful amidst the happy commerce I tell her,
"They're the sort that roam the plains with the buffalo;
"close thunder claps scare them."
"Like me," she says sympathetically.
"Right, and cowboys have to round them up when they stampede."
"They're chicken chickens," she says,
in the game now.

"But they're really smart," I say,
"they can spell hard words – like cacciatore and fricassee."
"But those words scare them, too,"
says my wise little free-range chick.

Geography

Baby Ruths cost a nickel when
I went to school in a red brick box
unimaginatively named for a low number as if
no dead mayor or departed pedagogue
merited such honor.

The alphabet in script -- capitals and lower case
stretched above the blackboard
to inspire perfect penmanship.

The big world map on our fourth-grade wall
was shaded mostly red for the vast British Empire
in geography kids giggled
when they answered Timbuktu or Popocatepetl
and again when we learned
Eskimos on Baffin Island ate blubber
The word rolled off our tongues,
round as those exemplary Os
above the blackboard.

Apples

They give up their warm bed
    at five-fifteen this morning
she scrambles eggs, he brews coffee
they leave the kitchen clean and warm
for their two girls and her mother
    still sleeping

he filled the van last night
    with the orchard's stored harvest
they're taking to the farmers' market
an hour away in the city
past fields splashed with leftover snow
    like bed sheets blown from a clothesline

in this capricious passage between
    stubborn winter and evasive spring
when fetal fruit's at risk he attends their trees
as a nurse tends rows of preemies
wondering if they should dare experiment with
    figs foreign to this unruly climate

under a glacier-blue sky they occupy
    their appointed space greeted by smells of
midnight-baked bread from the next stand
he stacks bushels of fruit --- Pink Lady, Braeburn,
Fuji, Honeycrisp, Goldrush --- jugs of cider, jars of apple butter
    apple sauce she slices samples --- sweet, tart, winey

hundreds of varieties of apples
    adorn the world what kind
        got Adam exiled
        caught Tell's arrow
        struck Newton's curiosity
        sat still for Cézanne?

each variety has a story
    its genealogy   "Three kinds will
make a nice pie," she answers a customer
at three it grows quiet they reload the van – lighter now
its radio warns of an overnight freeze.

Sea of Corn

Well into August the corn
   stands over my head
stalks straight fibrous dense
   as a bamboo thicket
flooding the fields along our county road

on my morning walk
   before the day's full heat
I hear stirring in the green maize, likely
the doe and her fawn I've glimpsed
   between woods and fields

Albert Morris rents these acres
   from folks like me too old now
to still work the land ourselves
most of the year he's running
   the hardware in town

but a few days each spring
we see him on his John Deere
   sowing seed and later
towing tanks of fertilizer back-and-forth
   back-and-forth like a weaver at the loom

after Labor Day Albert will be back
   high in the cab of his harvester
sailing through this sea of corn

so much bounty from
one man's industry, his machines
persistent science, providential Nature

the loaves and fishes
along our county road.

Usage

I like saying
Quotidian
it curls off my tongue
     like Dairy Queen
  into a sugar cone

inviting rhyming with, say,
   scythian or
   tyrian or maybe
   diluvian

But it can be an ungainly modifier;
who'd pray for our quotidian bread
       or
swallow a quotidian multivitamin
       or
sweat the quotidian dozen?

a synonym to apply
with restrained delight.

Spanish

Spanish is the language of
Cervantes and Neruda and Marquez

and of the undocumented who risk
crossing to the North in order to
remit to the South

of the sun-browned braceros
whose quick hands harvest our ripe fields

of the cheery Latina whose practiced hands gently turn
my mother in her hospital bed

of the nanny cell-phoning comfort
to her own ninos while shepherding
her fair-faced charges

of the boom-box music in the construction site dust

of the few scripted words
Anglo pols recite to sway
the majority minority from
whom may come a future president
or even a new Cervantes.

Brick Work

Raoul's hands are rough
    as the bricks he is laying
to build a wall between
our back yard and the neighbors'
replacing rusted-out fencing

The mortar his cousin Moises mixes
    in a crusted tub -
cement and sand watered
from a green garden hose – is
the texture and color of refried beans

Raoul trowels on the mortar
    like thick frosting on a wedding cake
binding bricks one-to-another straight
and plumb as the level's bubble he eyes requires
though not so elegant as Mr. Jefferson's winding wall

Finished our wall will be elbow-high
    a border but not a barrier
on summer afternoons we'll talk and
    laugh and pass cold beers over it
across the art of Raoul's hands.

McAvoy & Sons

At the end of the ladder
    stretched its full three stories to my roof
two thin men are silhouetted
    against the autumn sky

removing worn shingles, broken slates
    pitted metal, cracked flashing
materials gone frail allowing
rain or melting snow to drip
drip into a dishpan and old pots
in my bedroom and closet

this debridement precedes their
    sealing suspect seams, laying tarpaper
resetting shingles and slates

Church bell peals float with
    oak and maple leaves
across the housetops
the men's untucked shirttails flutter
    in the wind
they'll work til the edge
    of early dark
do they get butterflies or
bumblebees in their bellies
when the ladder sags as they climb,
    I wonder.

Inside the panel truck at the curb
    radio and heater on
sits their father who started
    the business before they were born
muscling buckets of hot pitch heavenward
he lowers his window emitting
    a wave of cigar smoke

he thanks me for the check I hand him
I thank him for his boys' good work
grateful I can go inside and
put away the old pots and dishpan.

The Med Student

Along pale gray hospital corridors
        busy with healing traffic
she gravitates in a scrum of classmates
from bedside to bedside attentive
to their mentor's manner
stethoscope bobbing against
      her crisp white coat
instrument and cloak of authority

exuding youthful vitality
amidst geriatric frailty and pained flesh
apprentice to a millennia-old calling
      older than Hippocrates and Galen
practiced with priestly incantations,
        earth's balms, desperate purges, touch.

the armamentarium
      to be one day at her summons
bears a wondrous apothecary
and savvy devices so she can spy
      on excited synapses or
spelunk inside the body's caverns

she sees despairing loss, unordained recovery
as she acquires the power of possibilities
the grace of limits.

September Song

If we could have slipped
    past blue-green summer hid

behind three full moons or had
    blindfolded fate

if innocent flesh had not
    turned savage thwarted

the healers who could offer only
    solace not commutation

your few tears anointed my lips
    you braver than me

unloosed then from lines like a ship
    casting off for an unknown sea

First of January

Closing the front door
    on caressing warmth
jacket zipped against dark cold
my face feels
    the promise of snow

the only sound like
    crumpling Christmas wrapping
lacy ice crunching underfoot
until through the unfrocked trees
I hear an aria, my neighbors' beagle

last night they mixed Old Fashioneds and
we drank to present ghosts

first flakes falling
I walk a quarter mile to
    where gravel meets macadam
then back to fix
a cup of instant coffee.

Man on the Porch

He sits on the back porch in
    the rising dark,
telling himself stories or
    humming songs whose lyrics
        sweeten the still air

The arriving full moon looks
    to him like a communion wafer

What's left of the day is
    a low rail of light, a
        wall between memory and mystery.

Make-believe

Charlie Chaplin
Once on a lark
Entered a Charlie Chaplin look-alike contest
-- and lost.

Was pseudo Charlie
    a better mime?
could the star's leading ladies
    detect the stand-in from their lover,
the starving tramp
eating his shoelaces like spaghetti,
his shoes like savory beef?

Would you choose ersatz over genuine
a paper moon or the real McCoy reflected on the sea
wax blossoms or spring daffodils
comforting illusion or disquieting truth?

Encoded

They
    who are They?
know so much about me
my DOB, DNA, bank balance
my shoe size, favorite cereal, my politics

I am zip-coded, area-coded, color-coded
credit-scored, polled and pigeon-holed
enumerated decennially -- Moses didn't ask
    so many questions
        counting his people in Sinai

I am watchable making coffee or making love
by a Monarch-size snoop at the window
I am data points --
    like dots in a pointillist's
        portrait of me
cached in the Cloud

Well They know my IQ
    but not my mind
my heart rate
    but not my heart

Not yet.

Judgment

Summoned
    past auction of forlorn homes
    between starling-stained pillars
for civic duty vetted and sworn

Cast
    in roles they've studied in
    prime time, but their verdict unscripted
twelve women and men quite ordinary

Instructed
    to peer through gray shadows
    veiling doubt and belief
to let hearts and heads clash

Chambered
    like storm-delayed travelers
    bound together just once to
find acceptable truth.

The Little Lizard

Shimmering green as the South China Sea
the little lizard scurried
across the window screen
to escape my Samaritan fingers
their pulse now ensnared
with the tiny dragon's heartbeat.

I gently lifted it from the wire mesh
to assumed shelter in the tall wet grass
among its own.

But night-stalking frogs and predatory snakes
and, yes, kin-eating lizards and overhead raptors
feed in this mini Jurassic Park.

I have not seen the little lizard
since doing it a good turn.

Old San Juan

In a sultry midnight
we sit at an open window
of our upper floor tryst
in El Convento
hearing an accordion from
the garden of La Fortaleza
    we'd rather hear Casals' cello

we watch the ferry's starry wake
    cross the harbor
Antillean breezes
cool our enfolded selves
awaiting a rapture we doubt
the departed Carmelites
could neither know nor envy.

Penmanship

Pressed between my fingers
my fountain pen
heir of the graceful quill

seems to be an extension of self
like a tailor's needle
    a surgeon's scalpel

uncapped nib gliding on paper
blue-black revelations
indelible pledge of love.

A Matter of Vowels

Live and love
so close, one so like the other
the O like the pucker inviting a kiss
the I slender as a ring finger.

Confluence

I saw my ex
across the street this afternoon

a shopping bag in each hand
when the light changed

I crossed to her side

took both bags

and kissed her surprised lips

Evidence of Love

I tell you I love you but you say prove it
How? I say -- Send me roses when
    it's not my birthday, you say
drop the keys to a frisky red Ferrari
in my pleased palm, a long weekend
    at a spa'd be nice, you say

I do love you, I say -- so
come smell the summer night
see the stars blowing kisses
share this frolicky Italian red
let me rub your bare back
doesn't this prove something? I say

Maui

Far up the exalted slopes
    of sleeping Haleakala
my love and I passed a time
in a cottage laced by
    protea and bird of paradise
feasting from a mango tree
    branching over our roof until

bewitched one night
    by the Southern Cross
we trembled at the lanai's edge
naked, drawn to leap
    arms like wings
into the enveloping shimmer
    not like defiant Icarus

and sail downward in rapturous tacks
over red-earth fields
    of cane and pine
toward Kahoolawe's palisades
    and maternal waves
where Maui
    and her sisters had spawned.

The Dancer

Beneath the overhead fan's circling
    blades in time with my heartbeat
you dance to the music of Eastern winds

dark hair falls to your waist
chemise the color of cinnamon
    hitched to your knees
bare feet on bare wood moving
    in unlaced freedom

I touch cold desert sand, I am burned
    by hot stars
I embrace the haze, I taste Salomé

uncertain whether I am
    refreshed by an oasis spring
or made drunk by a mirage.

Loggerheads

Summer houses' seaside lights
    are doused when
loggerheads are due to hatch
    from nests between dune and surf
lest incandescence lure
these millennia-old newborns
inland where raccoons and foxes hunger

shells shimmering slick
    as just-washed china
the turtles -- half-dollar round
waddle along starshine and moonglow
into the waves around the shoals
    parting estuary from sea
on their perilous predestined swim
to an Atlantic somewhere

in late afternoon first shadows
    fill empty loggerhead nests
barnacled pilings lean
    like dozing sentinels
the slipping sun turns water gold
careened in sand worm-augured keel and ribs
    of an unrecalled little sloop await
another storm to compel it rudderless
to an Atlantic somewhere.

Masts

Bound for the sawmill
stacked like pick-up-sticks
the limbless pines
    that last night
seemed to pierce the low clouds
lie the length of the flatbed
    and then some,
straining at their chains
longing to be the stout masts
    of a flotilla of tall ships
bound for the open sea.

Navigation

1
Somewhere I read that
Polynesian paddlers
followed the Golden Plover
to find Hawaii and
the soaring Frigate to discover New Zealand

2
Cottony clouds coast across
my sliding glass doors
reflections promising passage
to endless skies

3
Over the wind chimes' song
I hear a muffled thump
winged life defeated
by the clarity of illusion

4
I lift the bird light as a handful of blueberries then
Alive! and gone in a slate-gray blur
to winter among Mayan bones

5
Pequod steered by the sun and stars
Kon Tiki sailed on easterly currents
What compass guides my voyage?

Crossing Bay Bridge

swaddled in grayness
its companion span spectral as the gulls glide

beneath and between laced girders
lifted from some giant Erector Set

over the Chesapeake without horizon
the old ferry'd never sail in such soup

in grayness - uncertainty's shade
the unblinking tail lights of the car ahead

are reassuring when
the sun is so timid

Birthday Girl

Annalee turned one hundred today
eyes blue -- bright but unseeing
she grasps little of her yesterdays
perhaps an anodynic blessing
small hands restless on her
        wheelchair's arms

grandchildren and their children
study those hands.
they cue her to puff out
        the celebratory candles
Make a wish, they chant.
at one hundred what's there to wish for?
she smiles at the first
sugary bite of birthday cake.

Remembering Annalee Bird Blessing

Tightrope Walking

*Grow old along with me
the best is yet to be,*
beckons Rabbi Ben Ezra.

Really? The best?
    I challenge Browning's sage

When
    your kids impound your car keys
    the second floor feels like K-2
    lust sags winter drags summer races
    weeds outgrow roses
    dreams retreat, friends become eulogies

But on the other hand, Ben Ezra responds
There's
    yoga, preboarding
    Dr. Fixit mends knees, takes a tuck
    dispenses bedroom potions
    laughter is gold, wisdom is possible
    revivals are staged

Enough now, Rabbi
let's drop this Talmudic balancing act
time's short!
just bless us up here on the high wire

The Oak

our neighborhood's oldest living resident
six maybe seven generations, the arborist figures

its height humbling homes
vital (knock on wood) unlike
blighted chestnut and elm

tenant squirrels scramble up and down
the rivuletted trunk aimlessly, it seems
except in fall's frenetic foraging for fat
acorns, their abundance foretelling hard winter
when winds worry its geriatric joints

in spring it opens its sun-splashed sail, spread
like a sheltering beach umbrella
catching kids' laughter as a bough-gripped
swing propels them toward freedom

when sudden summer storms startle
we here below entreat Mother Earth
to hug tight for all seasons

the oak

Ambience

Through midnight-dark woods
along marshes awake with
    night-needing life
the river lies pale, seducing

starlight, a sliver of new moon
eyes and skin of an acrobatic bass
lamp glow at the end of the dock
reflected hull of the snugged Whaler

current luring light
light spilling onto water
like falling in love.

Along the River

The platinum sun defers its warmth,
where it touches the river
   votive candles flicker

around the silent rental shack
overturned canoes and kayaks huddle
   like the parish faithful

waiting

with the black-cloaked cormorants
cloistered in the
   leafless steeple-high sycamore

on the low bank nudging infant ice
a great blue heron finds me
   with its angler eye, together
we genuflect in this wall less cathedral

waiting

for the yellow sun.

Crew

Out of the lifting morning mist
the eight oarsmen,
    bent like monks at prayer,
slowly propel their shell
    slender as a lance,
away from the boathouse dock
in a graceful arc

toward the starting line buoy
    at the center of the river
blades barely denting the flat water
    barely trailing a wake
at the stern the coxswain,
    lithe as a birch sapling,
perches like an afterthought.

At the buoy the rowers'
outstretched oars hold the eight steady
    anticipating the coxswain's command
"Row!"

Oars beat metronomically
the shell sprints downstream
breaks the river's grip
and rises toward the low sun

    geese gawk
    gulls giggle
    mallards marvel

the coxswain raises his fist high
pumped for tomorrow's regatta.

Social Media

Convened restlessly high in the loblolly pines
the crows interrupt their matinal caw-cawphony
to surveil me approaching on the damp needles

but only for a moment and then they resume
their party-line deliberations about
fresh road kill and the nearing rain

and the circling hawk's intentions
all far more urgent than anything
on my ordinary mind

A Cat Tale

Prowling past
    trash and recycle bins
around faded azaleas
Mrs. Keats' cat halts,
      belly bending sun-warmed grass
mischief or mayhem --
I can't tell which --
in his eye, transfixed
on an insouciant squirrel,
its tail cavorting like smoke in a breeze,
scavenging for thistle seed
fallen from the finch feeder

For a moment
my expeditionary eye watches
a big cat stalk an incautious gnu
on the Serengeti Plain

And then Mrs. Keats' cat --
    his calculations completed --
        pounces!
the squirrel catapults to its haven oak
its giddy chp-chps taunt
Mrs. Keats' kitty,
killer or clown?

Max

Sheltered
but on life's short leash
belly worm-swollen, quirky tail
    longer than your puppy body
fitful eyes pleading with ours

so we brought you home
expectantly named you Maximus
scrubbed until your chocolate coat shone
nursed you well, taught you manners --
    you kept a truce with the next-door tom
cold nights you made our bed yours

years now since that first love
you past cure but not pain
the vet's welcome needle withdrawn
you lay across our laps, fading breath
   dry on our wet cheeks
sheltered   still.

Phone Call

The nearest pay phone
stood outside Levy's Drugs
two blocks from my house
one autumn night avoiding
the telephone on our kitchen wall
    my mother's amusement
    my father's impatience
    my big sister's big ears
I stepped furtively as a secret agent
      inside that phone booth
hardly more than a broom closet
smelling of cigarette smoke
I pulled shut the accordion door
placed the receiver at my ear
dropped a nickel into the coin slot
and ever-so-slowly dialed
a well-studied number
    wishing for a saving busy signal
    wishing to hear her answer
    fearing to hang up if I heard her
      "Hello"
wondering if the booth's grimy glass
  hid my agony from passersby.

Though the phone booth and Levy's
are gone, her number clings to my finger tip.

Home Ec

My mother's Singer stood
    on dependable legs
    at her bedroom window
the white chintz curtains her doing

Shoulders a little hunched she sat
    right foot compressing treadle
    transfusing her energy as
a trumpeter's breath animates his horn

Her long fingers so cool
    on a feverish child's cheek
    guide cloth to eager needle
threaded from jiggling spool

Such purposeful clatter yields
    apparel practical – and smart
    from patterns scissored pieces
spread like leaves on her bed

One June night my big sister
    went off aglow to her prom
    in a lilac chiffon formal
our mother had just finished hemming

My mother's Singer stands
    awaiting disposition
    machine silent as its mistress
a stitch in time their perfect harmony.

Catching Flies

In flashes of angry heat
good sense and reasonableness boiling away
my mother's recollected counsel cools,
"You can catch more flies
with honey than with vinegar."

it works sometimes
my mother's aphorism nudging
    toward remedy.

But in summer's stillness
I couldn't count so many flies
    some still quivering
trapped on the unsweetened strip
she'd hung from the kitchen ceiling.

My mother, a practical woman,
also told me
"There's more than one way to skin a cat."

Or a fly.

Obit

The News died today,
its presses' rolling thunder stilled,
another newspaper the Constitution guaranteed freedom
but not eternity,
pulled under by unrelenting tides

interred in journalism's boneyard
beneath tombstones inscribed
The Globe, The Star, The Sun,
bold flags that described their aspired reach,
The Herald, The Courier, The Examiner
their proclaimed missions aborted

The News died today,
archived with gone broadsheets and tabloids
-- like the Dead Sea Scrolls --
for revelations of sins petty and profound,
of momentary idols, alarms ignored
official lies and trickling truths

"The first rough draft of history"
a publisher said of each day's stories
once gathered by telegraph, telephone and shoe leather
from familiar and exotic places
long before a clever mouse could summon worlds.

City Limits

How doth the city sit solitary
                 -- Lamentations

Main Street shops idled behind dust-webbed glass
decent folks in prim ranchers
     await the evening news
Sabbath-keepers abide in vestigial hope
the old mill hands with remembering eyes benched
     in the shadows of the padlocked depot

the young wait at the by-pass for
   the Greyhound to elsewhere
among runaway hubcaps and drained soda cans
18-wheelers drown the midnight insects' songs
the young exported like the mill hands' labor

the town done in not by
unquenchable thirst like an Anasazi pueblo
nor by played-out veins of ore
calamitous Nature nor wrathful men
the town suffocated by indifferent Time.

Yard Sale

Our leafy souk displays thirty years of
possessions now surplus to our downsized lives:

100 feet of snake-coiled garden
hose, paperbacks, read but not

abandoned in beach rentals and coach-class
seats; six large bowls with flawed

glazes from a dear friend's kiln, a tin
roofed bird house claimed by wrens through

twenty springs; an easel from your
dabble in watercolors; the child's

dresser you first painted blue and later
pink; the guitar for which I had the taste

but not the touch; two wicker chairs from
which we watched the summer sun go

down a hundred million miles
beyond the dogwoods---

Let's buy it all back, you say though
we both know that everything must go---

the Pawley's Island hammock where
we lay so many cooling
darks counting and counting

still farther stars.

Summerset Review (Summer 2013) previously published this poem.

The DC-3

Wearing helmet and goggles
    imitating Lindy's
the boy studied the airplane
    its twin propellers stilled
a DC-3 he was sure he
watched luggage and mail sacks stowed
watched passengers duck through

    the narrow door and up
the canted aisle between twenty-one seats
almost a day with stops
    coast-to-coast
only his father's hand stayed him
    from running to touch silvery skin

At the darkened movies before
    cartoons and cowboys the boy
watched newsreels of brave men
    parachuting from echelons of
DC-3s now repainted olive drab
with big white stars on wings and fuselage
pretending he was at the controls

A gray-haired man boyishly surprised
sees the airplane -- graceful as ever
standing on the airport tarmac
he finally touches silvery remembrance

Conducting Heat

Over our shoulders
the thermostat I've set quite low
    risking our marriage to rescue the planet
clicks on as if it too hears
    the pretty weather woman forecast
fall's first frost.

below us the old furnace ends
its long idleness -- responsive pipes
    and valves become drums, a bass, a bassoon
Stravinsky composing in the basement

in a while a radiant OOOMMM
    shrouds the discordant notes
warming us, saving our union.

Cadence

In still-stiff combat boots
rousted by non-coms' shouted commands
    "Move! Move!"
we spill from the slight warmth of
bare-walled barracks
possibly occupied not long before
by our older brothers or uncles
    destined for the Big War

Now we are taking our turn for new battles
    beyond our geography lessons
160 recruits of Baker Company
in chill pre-dawn
    smelling of coal smoke and autumn
marching in twos along a red clay road
    to the rifle range
led by First Sergeant Gentry who,
    as lean light shimmers,
begins chanting cadence in his Carolina drawl
we see our echoing breaths.

    I don't know but I've been told
    in Korea it's mighty cold

Prone on hard ground
we load, aim and fire our rifles
    at far targets
over and over again
filling the air with cordite's acrid bite
repeatedly we clean and oil our piece
slipping a condom over the muzzle
    when rain threatens
in bivouacs we sleep snug
with our semi-automatic lover

I got a gal who lives on a hill
She won't but her sister will

One moonless night
    thin frost scaling the land
we snake through barbed wire
toward a mock enemy
flare bursts snare us in momentary daylight
tracers – like crazed fireflies –
    streak over our hunched bodies
we read compasses by dimmed flashlights
    to find our way
all just like the movies

You get a line and I'll get a pole
And we'll go down to the crawdad hole

Over dwindling weeks
we launch rockets at decaying tanks
    cheer each hit on the steel corpses
buddies boost each other over mean barricades
    to thrust bayonets into straw men's bellies
we staunch pretend wounds, splint healthy limbs,
rehearsing.

Now on a fall early morning
I hear on the wind
Sergeant Gentry and Baker Company again
counting cadence
counting cadence
dreading winter.

Dover

Eastward
the giant jet beating
against dark clouds loud
    as ten thousand chariots
bore this young warrior
spent by the captain memoryless
    of Santayana's prophecy
to a hard land where
    imperial Alexander had lost his way

Westward
now descending over squandered
    abundance, over Delmarva's distracted pleasures
the bird bears him riven
unseen to Dover's cradling hands.

The U.S. military mortuary is at Dover (Del.) Air Force Base

Arlington Section 60

Shoulder-to-shoulder
as if obedient to the last tattoo

they lie in this fresh meadow
in every weather so---so many

early sun warms the back
of a young woman kneeling

by her husband's stone testament
a boy and girl each leave a rose

in the shade of bordering trees
a mother and father lay hands

on their child's spare tablet

May breezes ripple rows of flags
they wave and wave

on this mourning day
before noon.

Faces

They cover two pages of today's newspaper
ninety-nine faces a few bare facts beneath each
      resembling a high school yearbook
in eleven rows of nine as though
the editor commanded they fall
into squads for this final formation

who will pause to study these young faces?
America's dead from only fifty-nine days
    of our forever follies
in two dismembered lands

one soldier rests his cheek on his dog's head,
    halfway home he died of battle wounds
makeshift, but not amateurish, bombs killed forty-one
      ambushes another eight
a Marine was swept away helping
    an Afghan cross the Helmand River
many of them smile, the lone woman beams
    a rocket ended her life at twenty-three

who will pause to study these young faces
before turning to yesterday's calamities
tonight's entertainments?

The Washington Post published the 99 photos August 19, 2010.

Sic Transit

The trestle spans a shadowed ravine
anchored by concrete piers
streaked ochre from rusting beams
    like old spilled blood
webbed with honeysuckle, ivy, wisteria

silent until
high winds prompt
    splintered planks to moan
stripped of the rails
    streetcars clattered on
to the fun park

whose unlatched laughter
sticks like cotton candy
    to the wild rides
now tamed and derelict
as the trestle.

Stone Saints

Stone wrenched from grieving earth
stone transfused with rebellious blood
rock of ages cleft for images of
mere mortals, not of Hellenic Zeus or Rome's god-men

Here on the tidal river shore
enthroned Lincoln weeps stone tears
for the legions the land had sacrificed for
the Union's salvation and freedom's rebirth

Near him bare to sun and storm sits King
who mustered multitudes in freedom's cause and
like Lincoln martyred
by a hate-borne bullet

Close stands pedastaled Jefferson
whose testament gloriously rang of man's
unalienable right to liberty while
slaves sustained his bountiful Monticello

In quiet after pilgrims and day depart
Lincoln ponders the price of freedom
Jefferson stirs in King's pastoral gaze
they meditate on the elusive reality of dreams
the frailty of stone.

Prayer

Pray for rain
    Comes coiled thunder

Beseech the storm abate
    Its anger rises

Long for quiet
    Hear despairing silence

Ask for light
    Light blinds

Plead for truth
    Whose truth?

Court love
    Love escapes

Yearn for faith
    Doubt vamps the soul

Seek a sign
    The screen fades to black

Reach for God's ear
    God takes a long lunch

Aridzona

Above the saguaro
up in the ponderosa pines
the prancing light I first
believe is moonglow I realize
is a cabin in flames

the downwind blowing embers
yellow as a coyote's eyes
into the dry wash where
I'd seen a bobcat teaching her kit
    to hunt in the brush
fire when we burn for rain.

Public Library

I finished the morning paper in the public library
and went into the men's to take a leak
a wiry man -- only his face familiar to me --
stood totally naked at the lone sink

giving himself a wash
with cold water and liquid soap
drying off with wads of rough paper towels
all free as the newspaper I had just read
he ignored me
I concentrated on the urinal wall

I've seen him occasionally this winter
bent over *The Wall Street Journal* or
    The Financial Times or *Fortune*
his shaggy head sometimes
   resting on the spread pages

he returns from his ablution and
takes The Economist to the end of
    the long oak table we share
I watch him peripherally,
he appears worn but younger than me
not yet entitled, like me
   to a Social Security check

I wonder if his apparent sorry state stems
from losing his job or investments tanking
maybe he's a genuine contrarian or simply a miser with
millions in blue chips and treasuries
or cash stashed in shoe boxes

perhaps I should invite him for coffee and a bun
   at the corner shop ask his thoughts on
the Euro's fate, the yen's rate

quantitative easing or credit default swaps
I'd expect him to be nakedly honest.

Two A.M.

Sleepless
at two in the middle-America morning
I turn on the bedside radio for company
and hear the assured BBC anchor
in breakfast-time London
chronicling turmoil in
Kigali and Kirkuk, Kum and Kandahar.

In the half-darkened world
sound travels faster than light.
I drift off, grateful
Keokuk and Kokomo, Kankakee and Kalamazoo
do not attract BBC's notice this day.